British Railways Pict

Leicestershire and Rutland

David Webb

Ian Allan

PUBLISHING

CONTENTS

First published 2007

ISBN (10) 0 7110 3219 X
ISBN (13) 978 0 7110 3219 4

Published by Ian Allan Publishing

an imprint of Ian Allan Publishing Ltd,
Hersham, Surrey KT12 4RG
Printed in England by Ian Allan Printing Ltd,
Hersham, Surrey KT12 4RG

Code: 0711/B1

Visit the Ian Allan Publishing website at
www.ianallanpublishing.com

AUTHOR'S NOTE

This book brings together the work of three photographers from Leicester. The vast majority of their pictures are from the years 1947-63 and are a record of many everyday railway scenes in Leicestershire and Rutland. They are all from the cameras of the late John Mervyn Mason, his brother Michael Mason, and the author, David Webb. All three grew up in an age when steam railways provided the principal means of medium- and long-distance transport for people and commerce. Fortunately they used their opportunities to record what they saw, and this book will re-create those scenes for everyone to savour.

Particular care has been taken to include, wherever possible, pictures that show the complete railway scene, with the infrastructure intact, long before rationalisation, modernisation and, in many cases, closure.

It has obviously not been possible to cover every part of this once very extensive and busy network of railway lines. However, the views selected show very representative examples of both main-line and branch-line railways from the two counties.

All the pictures in this book were taken when the railway authorities were far more relaxed about the 'health and safety' aspects of railway photography. Lineside photographic permits were held by all three photographers and covered the locations seen here.

My thanks must go to my friends Horace Gamble, Robin Cullup and Michael Mason for their help, in various ways, while I was gathering material for this book.

Front cover: Double-chimney Class 9F 2-10-0 No 92231 climbs away from Leicester with an up freight from Annesley to Woodford Halse in the summer of 1963. *J. M. Mason*

Back cover, top: Class 4F 0-6-0 No 44414 at Seaton on 18 May 1963, waiting to be attached to the rear of an RCTS special, about to go up to Uppingham as part of a branch-line tour. *D. W. Webb*

Back cover, middle: Class B1 No 61177 on a Skegness excursion passing Forest Road Crossing, Leicester, in the summer of 1960. *D. W. Webb*

Back cover, bottom: Bagworth Colliery Peckett 0-6-0ST No 1404 of 1915, bringing empty wagons up to the colliery, is about to cross the road from Bagworth to Ellistown on 6 November 1965. *J. M. Mason*

Title page:
Class O1 No 63808 gathers speed after its water stop on the up goods loop at Leicester South Goods on 1 October 1950. The signal is 'off' for the train to cross to the up fast line in a few more yards. The other arms on this bracket signal are for access to the engine shed, shunting yard and the long siding, which was parallel to the down goods loop. *J. M. Mason*

INTRODUCTION

The railways of Great Britain were changed for ever by two Acts of Parliament, the first leading to the Grouping of 1923 and the second to Nationalisation in 1948.

On 1 January 1923 all the large and small British main-line railways were grouped to form just four big railway companies, mainly on a geographical basis. In Leicestershire, the companies involved in the formation of the London Midland & Scottish Railway (LMS) were the Midland Railway (MR) and the London & North Western Railway (LNWR). Likewise, the Great Northern Railway (GNR) and Great Central Railway (GCR) became part of the new London & North Eastern Railway (LNER). Gradually the new companies introduced new locomotives, rolling-stock and standardised procedures, but in the main the lines retained their pre-Grouping flavours.

The Nationalisation of the railways on 1 January 1948 had little immediate impact in Leicestershire and Rutland. The lines formerly owned by the LMS became part of the London Midland Region of the new British Railways, and those of the LNER part of the Eastern Region. In some cases, locomotives and stock ran for several years with no change to their numbering or previous owners' lettering. Passenger locomotives tended to be renumbered and to carry 'British Railways' in full fairly soon, long before standard liveries and a suitable crest were chosen, no doubt because they were in the public eye. On many engines, a large capital 'E' or 'M' was added above or beside their numbers, prior to proper renumbering.

Experimental liveries for both engines and coaches appeared on trains through Leicestershire in the summer of 1948. Eventually, express trains were in the chosen standardised crimson and cream, while coaches used on local trains were just red. However, it was still possible to see main-line coaches in full LMS livery with an 'M' prefix into the 1950s. Similarly, the LNER's varnished teak coach livery was still quite common well into the early 1950s at both Leicester Central and Belgrave Road stations.

Below:
Class 2P 4-4-0 No M536 passes Cattle Market Sidings on a local to Burton-upon-Trent. Seen on 7 June 1949, the engine is in early British Railways condition. A line of empty cattle trucks is in the siding on the left. *J. M. Mason*

Above:
On 7 May 1949 Class O1 2-8-0 No 63594 climbs steadily on the long gradient near Ashby Magna with an up freight on the old GCR line. The engine is in the first renumbered condition, before number plates and crests were introduced. The train is passing over the Wigston to Rugby line of the former Midland Railway – the parapet of the bridge is on the left.
J. M. Mason

Left:
'Britannia' class 4-6-2 No 70004 *William Shakespeare*, on a Manchester Central to London St Pancras express, is approaching Knighton Tunnel on 28 March 1959. The old Cattle Market ticket platform is on the left, and the up and down slow lines on the right.
J. M. Mason

Above:
Beyer-Garratt 2-6-6-2 No 47971 approaches Kibworth on the up fast line with a coal train from Toton Sidings to Wellingborough on 22 April 1954. *M. Mason*

Right:
Stanier '8F' 2-8-0 No 8027 is heading a long coal train on the up fast line at Wigston North Junction on 14 May 1949, still in LMS livery. *J. M. Mason*

Left:
A general view of Kibworth North Junction on 18 October 1958 shows the signalbox, track layout and Midland Railway signals. Standard '9F' No 92130 is on an up coal train. The up slow line from Wistow finished behind the engine. The down slow line on the left of the picture commenced at the previous signalbox at Kibworth station and continued to Wistow. *J. M. Mason*

Left:
A heavy up coal train from Annesley to Woodford Halse is just passing a searchlight Distant signal near Ashby Magna behind Class 9F 2-10-0 No 92089 on 28 March 1959. *M. Mason*

In 1939 the many privately owned coal wagons were pooled and became 'common-user'. They had previously been painted in their owners' chosen colours and in most cases carried conspicuous lettering. Many local Leicester coal firms had fleets of their own wagons at one time, and even into the late 1950s these former privately owned wooden vehicles could be seen regularly with most of their previous owners' names quite evident. However, the steady replacement of these old wagons saw them disappear from the local railway scene by the end of the period covered in this book.

In 1951 the first of the new BR Standard locomotives, the 'Britannia' class 4-6-2s, emerged from Crewe Works, but these were seen only rarely through Leicester until the end of the 1950s. Also in 1951 the first of the '73000' Class 5MT 4-6-0s were built at Derby, and these new engines took their turn with the normal 'Jubilees' and Class 5s on expresses through Leicester London Road. The chime whistles on these new engines made a pleasant change from the traditional ones heard at Leicester.

Finally, the last Standard design came out in 1954 as the first of the 251 members of the Class 9 2-10-0s. These were very successful on all duties and took over the fast service of coal trains from Annesley,

Nottingham, to Woodford Halse through Leicester Central. With the withdrawal of the LMS Beyer-Garratts in the late 1950s, the '9Fs' worked the heavy slow coal trains on the Midland main line jointly with the Class 8F 2-8-0s that pre-dated them by nearly 20 years.

At the end of 1947 the very first British main-line diesel locomotive, LMS No 10000, was built at Derby Works. It ran trials well into 1948 to London St Pancras and was seen daily at Leicester on expresses. It was, however, nearly 15 years before diesel locomotives took over all express trains through Leicester London Road.

1. EX-LMS LINES IN LEICESTERSHIRE

Throughout the whole of the late 1940s and well into the 1950s, few changes were seen in the local railway system, or in the traffic on the lines owned formerly by the LMS. Stations continued to serve the public and businesses, both in town and country, more or less as they had done since the dawn of railways. No matter how small the traffic, branch lines continued to feed the main lines as always.

Much of the traffic on the former Midland main line between Trent and Market Harborough passed through Leicestershire as part of its journey between more distant places. Express passenger trains ran between London St Pancras and towns and cities much further north: there were frequent trains to Manchester Central and Leeds, and some to Glasgow St Enoch and Edinburgh Waverley via the Leeds to Carlisle route. Generally few expresses started or terminated at Leicester London Road station, apart from special trains or day excursions. Overnight sleeping car expresses to and from Scotland passed through daily.

Local passenger trains operated quite an intensive service, calling at town and country stations on both the main line and the branches to Burton-upon-Trent, Nuneaton and Birmingham New Street, Rugby and Peterborough. Far fewer trains ran on Sundays, when some local stations were closed for the day.

Each year the start of the Summer Timetable was awaited eagerly by enthusiasts, as normal passenger services were augmented by a large number of holiday trains, mainly on Saturdays, to and from far-off destinations. In addition there were numerous day excursion trains to London, seaside resorts and many other places. All these were patronised very well, since few people owned private motor cars and rail travel was quite cheap and was generally quicker than by road.

Freight traffic was particularly heavy on the north-to-south main line. From Monday to Saturday there was always a constant procession of long coal trains going south and of empties returning north. Most of the coal traffic ran from Toton Sidings to Wellingborough, then on to London. A lot of ironstone was carried northwards from the Northamptonshire quarries around the Kettering area, going to ironworks at Stanton and in the Sheffield area.

Most country and branch-line stations had small goods yards, where local coal merchants had their coal delivered by the railway and other traffic was dealt with. Livestock could be accepted for travel in special trucks and many stations had animal pens on dedicated sidings. At Leicester, the Cattle Market had been built close to the main line, beside Welford Road, and there were special sidings there to handle the heavy livestock traffic that came in from all over the country on market days by cattle trains or in single trucks.

The country and branch-line goods yards were served daily by the 'pick-up' goods trains, which delivered full loads and took away empty wagons and loaded ones. There were several freight-only lines, some of which had enjoyed passenger services until 20 or 30 years earlier. The West Leicestershire Coalfield generated a lot of traffic, and there were some busy branch lines off the Leicester to Burton-upon-Trent line to carry this.

Several long-distance express goods trains ran to and from the large goods depot at Leicester. These vacuum-braked trains enabled goods to be carried at express speeds. They were used heavily, long before the days of the big articulated lorry

Right:
'Royal Scot' class 4-6-0 No 46101 *Royal Scots Grey* passes Wigston North Junction on an up Manchester express in May 1960. *J. M. Mason*

Above:

'Jubilee' class No 45605 *Cyprus* is on an up express. The Midland Railway lower-quadrant signal is the down fast line Starter for Wigston North Junction. In the distance behind it are the down Distants for Aylestone Junction. A new colour light signal replaced this stop signal to dispense with it and the Distants a year or two later. *M. Mason*

Left:

Judging by the dark exhaust from 'Jubilee' No 45739 *Ulster*, the loco fireman is hard at work. The train is an up Rugby League Cup Final special passing Knighton South Junction on 11 May 1963. A '4MT' class 2-6-0 is being held on the up slow line at the head of a coal train. The sidings in the triangle are being shunted by one of Leicester's '4F' 0-6-0s. The curving tracks on the left are the lines to and from Saffron Lane Junction, leading to the Burton-upon-Trent branch. *J. M. Mason*

Above:
Still in LMS livery, ex-Midland Class 2P No 456 is passing Cattle Market Sidings with a late-afternoon Leicester to Burton-upon-Trent local passenger train. The picture was taken 18 months after Nationalisation, on 14 June 1949. *J. M. Mason*

Below:
Ex-Midland Railway '4F' class 0-6-0 No 43894 is on a coal train on the up fast line between Aylestone Junction and Wigston North Junction on 5 March 1955. *M. Mason*

and the future motorway network. One particularly notable express goods ran in both directions every night, except Sunday evening, between Leicester and Carlisle. This resulted in one of the many Class 5s, 'Jubilee' 4-6-0s or 'Crab' 2-6-0s from Carlisle Kingmoor depot (68A) spending the day at Leicester before working back north that evening. This overnight train was unlikely to have been photographed, as it arrived in Leicester at just after 5am!

Two long-distance express passenger services ran from the Eastern Region through Leicester London Road every day from Monday to Saturday. Both were on their way to Birmingham New Street, and the first of the day was from Cleethorpes, via Nottingham Midland, and was hauled by one of Immingham's Class B1 4-6-0s. Until mid-1951 the engine was often in LNER livery of lined apple green, but with BR lettering and numbering. This train did not change engines at Leicester and the 'B1' ran right through to New Street. The whole train worked back to Cleethorpes in the early evening.

The other arrivals from the Eastern Region were from the old Midland & Great Northern (M&GN) section, with through coaches from Yarmouth Beach and Cromer Beach to New Street. Before World War II some M&GN engines had worked these trains right through to Leicester from South Lynn. During the period of this book ex-GER Class B12/3 4-6-0s and Class D16s were used, followed in the final years by Ivatt '4MT' 2-6-0s. For some years a very old GER coach acted as a refreshment car between South Lynn and Leicester, where it was kept in Campbell Street Sidings to await the returning train from Birmingham each afternoon. It was a regular afternoon spectacle to see two Ivatt 2-6-0s coupled together taking the train back to the east.

Left:
Smart in its new livery, Class 3F 0-6-0 No 43751 approaches Knighton New Tunnel with an up coal train on 12 April 1958. *M. Mason*

Left:
Wigston North Junction's Distants frame Class 8F No 48492 hauling an up coal train on 13 February 1958. The arms on the bracket are, from left to right, for the Hinckley, Rugby and Market Harborough lines. *D. W. Webb*

Right:
Ex-Midland Railway Class 4F 0-6-0 No 43933 is passing Cattle Market Sidings on a short freight. Several cattle trucks, which have brought in cattle earlier in the day, stand in and around the sidings. The skyline of Leicester had none of the later large office blocks or flats when photographed on 19 July 1958. *D. W. Webb*

Below:
Ex-LNER 'B1' class 4-6-0 No 61195, on the Cleethorpes to Birmingham New Street express, is leaving Knighton Tunnel on 1 May 1958. The engines on this working were based at Immingham depot (40B) and ran right through. They returned each evening on the train back to Cleethorpes. *M. Mason*

THE EX-LMS MAIN LINE THROUGH LEICESTERSHIRE

Once said to include the longest continuous stretch of four-track railway in the world, this route through central Leicestershire was developed in this form by the Midland Railway to handle a very heavy volume of traffic. In recent years the line has been reduced to three or even two tracks for some of its length, and to cope with modern methods of operation bi-directional running and new signalling have been introduced.

Prior to these changes, the four-track layout comprised the up and down fast lines on the western side and the up and down slow lines on the east, from Trent to Wigston North Junction. South of there, the slow lines were the two outside tracks and the fast lines the middle pair, as far as Kilby Bridge signalbox. This meant that the down slow line had to cross the two fast lines at Wigston North Junction, and down freight trains were often held there while they waited for a path across.

South of Kilby Bridge most of the remaining route through the county was double-track and became quite congested at times. There was a short section of four tracks again between Wistow and Kibworth, where slow freights, in either direction, could be held. Trains on this busy railway were controlled by many manually operated signalboxes, most of which dated back to Midland Railway days. These were all superseded by new power signalboxes at Leicester and Trent in recent times.

Close to the new Leicester Power Box, just to the north of London Road station, there was the large motive power depot, coded 15C, where around 80 steam locomotives were based. These were of many types and reflected the varied traffics handled on the railway.

On the main line from Trent to Market Harborough there were few notable engineering features. The only water troughs were just north of Loughborough, where trains were able to pick up water on a fast section of track. There were only two sets of tunnels. One was at Red Hill, just south of the bridge over the River Trent, where the passenger tunnel was 154 yards long and the parallel goods tunnel 167 yards. The other was just south of Cattle Market Sidings, Leicester, where Knighton Old and New tunnels were each 104 yards long. In recent years Knighton New Tunnel, which served the slow lines, has lost its tracks and stands empty.

Immediately south of Leicester station the route was more difficult to construct. The first quarter-mile started through a deep brick-walled cutting followed shortly afterwards by the Knighton Tunnels, then a long embankment and a deep, wide cutting all the way to Wigston North Junction.

There was once a locomotive depot at Wigston. This was a sub-shed of Leicester (15C), where engines that worked around the Wigston area were kept and surplus engines stored. In the early 1950s an ex-LT&SR 4-4-2 tank, No 41938, was stored in Wigston roundhouse. There was also a large busy shunting yard and a wagon repair works here, as well as several sidings where rakes of main-line carriages were kept.

From Wigston southwards the line climbed until just before Kibworth, which provided hard work for steam locomotives and their crews, before it ran steadily downhill most of the way to Market Harborough.

Returning to the north of Leicester many industrial concerns had their own private sidings along the route and were important railway customers; one such firm was a busy timber yard by Humberstone Road station. If there was no signalbox nearby, sidings had their own ground frames to work points and signals. Some siding owners had their own works shunting engines, amongst them Parker Plant, Richards Ironworks and Brush at Loughborough. At Mountsorrel Junction, between Barrow-upon-Soar and Sileby, an important private branch line to the Mountsorrel granite quarries left the main line, and continued westwards for a further 1½ miles to reach Swithland Sidings on the former GCR. Extensive exchange sidings were built for Mountsorrel stone traffic at both ends of the branch, and those at the former Mountsorrel Junction are still in use today, for the new stone terminal, although the branch line has been replaced by a conveyor belt. The small Hunslet steam engines that ran to here and worked at the quarries are long gone.

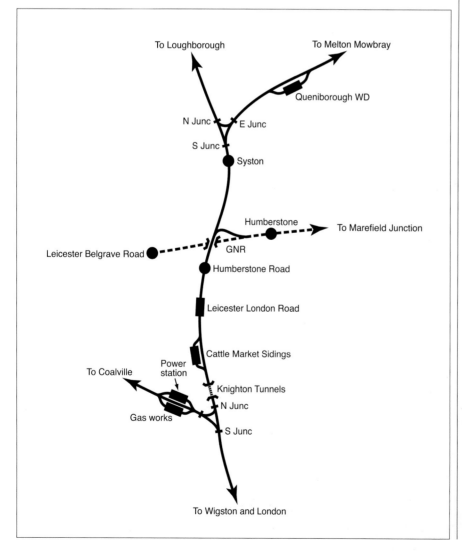

Right:
Class 8F 2-8-0 No 48704 crosses from the up fast to the up slow line at Syston North Junction. The line to Melton Mowbray and Peterborough diverged here to the east a few yards further on. The engine, which was allocated to Kettering (15B), was fresh out of shops when photographed on 12 October 1957. *D. W. Webb*

Left:
Ex-LMS Beyer-Garratt 2-6-6-2 No 47967 is on a long train of empty iron-ore tippler wagons on 12 October 1957. In the first picture it is about to take the Melton branch line at Syston North Junction. In the second it enters the curve towards Syston East Junction to head towards Melton Mowbray and the long way round to Kettering, with steam to spare. The rotary coal bunker can be seen clearly. At the time Beyer-Garratts, which were being withdrawn, were becoming rare. *Both D. W. Webb*

Above:
A pick-up freight from Melton Mowbray comes off the branch at Syston South Junction in October 1957, headed by Standard '2MT' No 78029. This short train is passing one of several long-surviving Midland Railway signals. *D. W. Webb*

Left:
'Britannia' class '7MT' No 70003 *John Bunyan* is on a Peterborough to Leicester train, and has just joined the main line from the branch at Syston South Junction on 19 May 1962. These engines were not usually seen on these workings, but on main-line expresses. The train is passing under the large gantry that spanned the fast lines. There is a water column on the left of the down slow line, and the Syston goods yard is being shunted on the right of the picture. *J. M. Mason*

Right:
Derby-based Class 8F 2-8-0 No 48168, on an up coal train, is passing Thurmaston box's up slow line Distant signal on 19 October 1957. The previous signalbox, Watkin's Siding, is in the far distance at the end of the train. *D. W. Webb*

Left:
'Claud Hamilton' Class D16/3 4-4-0 No 62599 passes under Humberstone Lane, Thurmaston, on a Leicester to Peterborough train on 11 August 1954. Several of these engines were at Peterborough Spital Bridge depot (35C) to work these trains. *M. Mason*

Right:
LMS Compound 4-4-0 No 40927 approaches Thurmaston at speed on an up local to Leicester on 31 March 1956. By this time withdrawals had started to reduce the class numbers and Compounds were not seen as frequently on the Midland main line. *M. Mason*

Above:
Leicester '4F' class 0-6-0 No 44231 hurries past Thurmaston signalbox on 30 August 1958. The train is a returning holiday special from Skegness and will have come via the M&GNR route between Spalding and Bourne. *D. W. Webb*

Left:
Ashwell & Nesbit's siding was just south of Thurmaston signalbox and was used for steel deliveries to this engineering works. Class 3F 0-6-0 No 43205 of Leicester 15C depot picks up an empty wagon on 12 October 1957; the rest of its train is waiting on the up slow line. The Home signal and points were worked from a ground frame, which also worked the up slow line Distant signal beneath Thurmaston's up Home signal. *D. W. Webb*

Above:
Fairbairn Class 3P 2-6-4 tank No 42160, with a Nottingham to Leicester local train, passes Parker Plant works at speed on 23 March 1958. The impressive bridge in the background went to nowhere on the right, but gave its name to the factory as 'The Viaduct Works'. *D. W. Webb*

Right:
Track workers stand back from their work for a moment as Class D16/3 No 62597 passes Humberstone Road Junction signalbox with a Peterborough to Leicester local in May 1959. Only the first carriage retains the earlier crimson and cream livery. In the background is the large Richards works, which had its own private siding and diesel locomotive. *D. W. Webb*

Left:
One of Leicester's five long-serving '3F' class 0-6-0 tanks, No 47543, pulls an empty steel plate wagon along the shunting line at Humberstone Road Junction on 6 May 1959; the wagon had been removed from Richards' private siding a few minutes earlier. *D. W. Webb*

Right:
Humberstone Road station is passed by a local from Peterborough hauled by 'D16/3' No 62613 on 13 June 1959. This engine was the last survivor of its class, being withdrawn in October 1960. The slow lines are behind the platform fence on the right. The sawmill in the background had its own siding with ground frame and stop signal, which was usually at clear. *J. M. Mason*

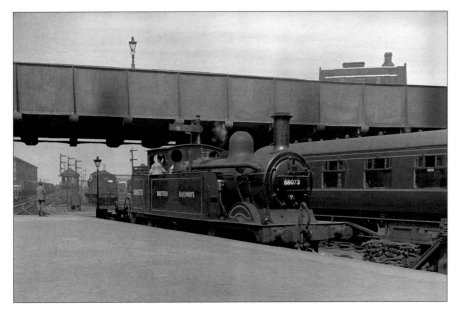

Left:
A busy scene at the north end of Platforms 1 and 2 at Leicester London Road station on 2 July 1949. For some years Johnson '1P' 0-4-4 tanks were used as station pilots until a new Ivatt 2-6-2 tank, No 41268, arrived in the early 1950s. No 58073 was one of the two pilots working on the day of the photograph, the other being No 58072, and it still carries condensing pipes from its days in the London area. The enormous goods warehouse can be seen on the left under Swain Street bridge, together with Leicester North signalbox and a '4F' 0-6-0. *J. M. Mason*

Right:
Another of Leicester's '3F' shunting tanks, No 47442, rests between shunting carriages in Campbell Street Sidings on 22 August 1959. *M. Mason*

Left:
South Lynn's 'B12/3' class 4-6-0 No 61540 has just taken over the Birmingham New Street to Yarmouth Beach afternoon train at Leicester London Road station on 15 April 1954. The engine has attached the South Lynn-based refreshment car from Campbell Street Sidings, where it stayed for a few hours while the main train made its journey to Birmingham and back. This car was always the front vehicle in the returning train. *M. Mason*

Right:
Ex-Midland '4P' 2-6-4 tank No 42330 passes Cattle Market Sidings on 9 October 1954. The splitting Distant arm is 'off' to show a clear road on to the Burton-upon-Trent line at Knighton North Junction. *M. Mason*

Left:
An up goods behind Class 8F 2-8-0 No 48390 passes the siding often used to store passenger carriages opposite Leicester Cattle Market. The Midland bracket signal, with its lower-quadrant arms, was replaced eventually by a modern steel bracket signal. *D. W. Webb*

Below:
One of the three original Beyer-Garratt 2-6-6-2s, No 47999, passes under Welford Road bridge on the up fast line on 12 March 1955. This engine was one of two that retained their fixed coal bunker. *M. Mason*

Right:
In 1946 the LMS introduced Class 2 2-6-0s, and one of the early engines, No 46404, is passing under Welford Road bridge with an afternoon local from Leicester to Wellingborough on 13 April 1962. *J. M. Mason*

Below:
Midland '3F' class 0-6-0 No 43728 emerges from Knighton New Tunnel with a down train of empty wagons on 12 April 1958. *M. Mason*

Left:
LMS 'Patriot' class 4-6-0 No 45542 leaves Knighton New Tunnel on a down freight from Nuneaton to Leicester on 5 August 1961. This member of the class was never named. *J. M. Mason*

Right:
Midland '2P' class 4-4-0 No 40439 leaves the south end of Knighton Tunnel on a Burton-upon-Trent local. The locomotive has an early British Railways livery in this view, taken on 26 June 1954. *M. Mason*

Left:
'Jubilee' class 4-6-0 No 45667 *Jellicoe* bursts out of the 104 yards of Knighton Tunnel on an up express on 27 April 1958. The complexity of the railway telegraph system can be seen by the number of insulators on the posts beside the signal. *M. Mason*

Right:
Ivatt '4MT' 2-6-0 No 43036 approaches Knighton North Junction on an up express on 4 August 1954. Both Knighton Tunnels can be seen clearly, with the slow lines going into the 'New' Tunnel on the right. *M. Mason*

Left:
Ex-LMS Beyer-Garratt 2-6-6-2 No 47988 is about to take the Burton-upon-Trent line at Knighton North Junction on 12 July 1954. This was a most unusual working for one of these engines, which normally ran directly from Toton to Wellingborough or London when passing through Leicester. *M. Mason*

Right:
On a particularly misty Saturday morning '8F' 2-8-0 No 48759 approaches Knighton South Junction on a down freight. The train, which is on the slow line, is passing the splitting Distant signals of Aylestone Junction signalbox, where trains could cross between the slow and the fast lines. The signal on the extreme right of the picture is the up main line Starter for Knighton South Junction and also carries Aylestone Junction's up main line Distant arm. *D. W. Webb*

Above:
A London express, its coaches all in crimson and cream livery, hurries through Wigston North Junction on 9 April 1955 behind Class 5 No 44861. This view gives a good idea of the width of the cutting, which was at least half a mile in length. *M. Mason*

Below:
A London to Manchester express is on the down fast line at Wigston North Junction in May 1960. 'Royal Scot' 4-6-0 No 46106 *Gordon Highlander* was unusual in having BR Standard smoke deflectors. Note the water column behind the signal, which was often used by freight locomotives when they were held here waiting for a path across the fast lines. *J. M. Mason*

Above:
A down freight train crosses the fast lines from the down slow on the west side to the down slow on the east side at Wigston North Junction on 14 May 1949. The locomotive is LMS '3F' 0-6-0 No 3522. The lines curving to the right are to Rugby and to Birmingham. *J. M. Mason*

Below:
A down empties behind '7F' 0-8-0 No 49293 is crossing the fast lines at Wigston North Junction on 26 April 1958. Note the many wagons in the sidings in the background, where shunting went on day and night. There were also wagon repair shops in the yard. *M. Mason*

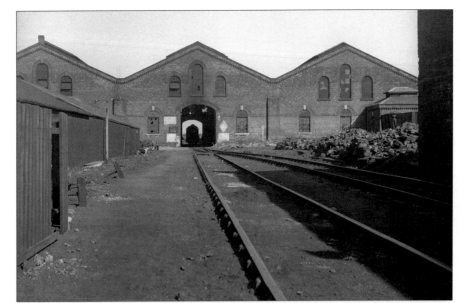

Left:
There was a locomotive shed at Wigston, which was a sub-depot to Leicester (15C) and was a single roundhouse with inside roads off a turntable. It was used by engines that worked in or from the Wigston area and also to store surplus locomotives. This view was taken on Saturday 22 April 1951. *J. M. Mason*

Left:
Inside Wigston roundhouse on the same day was ex-LT&SR 4-4-2 tank No 41938 and several Class 2P 4-4-0s, all of which were in store. There was also Class 8F No 48376, which was waiting for its next duties on the following Monday. *J. M. Mason*

Right:
The up slow line passed behind Wigston South Junction signalbox, and Class 8F 2-8-0 No 48005 is seen on an up train on 21 April 1954. This was one of the first 12 members of this numerous class that were built without domes in 1935. The fast lines and the down slow line are on the other side of the signalbox; the line nearest to the camera is a shunting line for the many wagon sidings to the right. *M. Mason*

Above:
Seen from the road bridge at Wigston Magna station on 6 May 1961, 'Jubilee' class 4-6-0 No 45649 *Hawkins* comes round the south curve to Wigston South Junction. The train is a Nuneaton to Wembley special and has just gained the up fast line. At other times, if the main line south of Nuneaton was blocked or closed, Euston-bound expresses would use this curve to reach the main line again south of Northampton, via Market Harborough. South Junction signal box is almost hidden by the steam and smoke. Coaching stock was stored in the sidings on the down side behind the train. *J. M. Mason*

Below:
Great Glen station, looking south from the road bridge, was originally named Glen station when opened in 1851; it was renamed in 1857 and closed finally in 1951. This picture, taken on 30 November 1959, eight years after closure to passengers, shows the track layout well, together with the signalbox and station buildings. There are several wagons of coal in the sidings, from which local coal merchants worked. The drive down to the station was on the left-hand side of the photograph. *D. W. Webb*

Left:
Returning to Wigston shed on a Saturday afternoon is ex-MR '2F' No 58305 and a brake-van. They are passing a building in the goods yard at Great Glen station used by local coal and animal feed merchants, Ellis & Everard Ltd. *D. W. Webb*

Left:
A down freight train is passing Great Glen signalbox behind two Class 9F 2-10-0s, Nos 92153 and 92156, in March 1959. A good mixture of coal wagons is seen in the goods yard. *J. M. Mason*

Right:
A down local passenger train hauled by Ivatt '4MT' 2-6-0 No 43012 passes the start of the loops at Kilby Bridge on 8 February 1958. This engine was fitted with a double chimney when built in 1948, but it was replaced by a single chimney a few years later. *D. W. Webb*

Right:
Former LNWR 0-8-0 No 48953 is on a down empties near Newton Harcourt, between Kilby Bridge and Kibworth, on 8 July 1959.
J. M. Mason

Left:
Former LNWR Compound 0-8-0 No 48915 was rebuilt in the early years of the LMS and is seen on an up coal train approaching Kibworth North Junction. The date is 18 September 1954.
M. Mason

Right:
Near Kibworth North Junction on 23 June 1961, Class 2 2-6-0 No 46496 speeds along on an up local passenger train. *M. Mason*

Left:
Down empty milk tanks are returning north headed by Class 5MT No 44861 near Kibworth on 3 June 1950. *J. M. Mason*

Right:
Kibworth North Junction is seen in the snow on 10 January 1959 as Class 4F 0-6-0 No 44164 heads a slow mixed freight southbound. One of the fine specimens of Midland Railway signals that abounded at Kibworth is in the background. *J. M. Mason*

Left:
A down excursion train hauled by LMS 'Crab' 2-6-0 No 42763 passes Kibworth North Junction on 3 June 1950. *J. M. Mason*

2. EX-LMS LEICESTERSHIRE BRANCHES

SYSTON TO PETERBOROUGH LINE

Just north of the site of Syston station, the Syston to Peterborough line heads east; to enable trains to join it from both directions a triangular junction was built and three signalboxes controlled the traffic. The branch line had many small country stations and level crossings. At Queniborough the WD built a large ordnance factory during World War II, with its own passenger station for the workers and several miles of internal railway. At first three Bagnall steam locomotives were employed, but later these were replaced by diesels. A new flat-roofed brick signalbox was built here to control WD traffic for the depot.

Between there and Melton Mowbray there were four stations along the Wreake Valley, at Rearsby, Brooksby, Frisby and Asfordby; the first and last closed in 1951, and the other two in 1961.

Shortly before Melton Mowbray station was Melton Junction, where a line from Nottingham joined the branch. This new line allowed express trains from the north to call at Nottingham, then run southwards without having to reverse. When opened in 1880 this line gave Melton Mowbray some express passenger trains to and from London St Pancras by a direct line through Manton; previously passengers had to change trains at Leicester. In 1967 the line from Nottingham was closed and for some years part of it was used as a railway test track.

Early in World War II the WD opened a large depot at Old Dalby, just 5 miles north-west of Melton Mowbray. This had rail access and there was a great deal of military traffic. There were three tunnels between Melton Junction and Old Dalby, at Asfordby (419 yards), Saxelby (543 yards) and Grimston (1,305 yards).

South of Manton the once heavily used route over the famous Welland Viaduct at Harringworth still joins the main line to London at Glendon South Junction, just north of Kettering. Many of the slow coal trains of years ago from Toton left the main line at Syston North Junction and went via Melton and this somewhat circuitous route, thus relieving pressure on the very busy direct line through Leicester. Long slow trains, hauled by Class 8F 2-8-0s and the unique LMS Beyer-Garratts, were a constant sight on the branch throughout the period covered by this book. East of Melton Mowbray there are still loop lines beside both main running lines as far as Brentingby, where there were once water troughs, much used in the days of steam.

A little further east, at Saxby station, just over 5 miles from Melton Mowbray, was Saxby Station Junction. Here at one time four tracks turned south towards Manton on their way towards Peterborough or Kettering, while the Midland Railway connection to the Midland & Great Northern (M&GN) at Little Bytham continued eastwards as a single track. Despite the complete closure of the entire M&GN system in 1959, part of this single line from Saxby remained in use for several more years to serve ironstone quarries at Market Overton, Buckminster and the short-lived Thistleton mine.

Right:
A Yarmouth Beach and Cromer Beach to Birmingham New Street train approaches Syston East Junction on 22 March 1958. The engine, No 43080, was one of a batch of Ivatt 2-6-0s that went brand new to the M&GN section to replace older ex-GER classes. They were all equipped with tablet-exchanging apparatus so that they could work over the many single-line sections at express speeds. *D. W. Webb*

Left:
LMS Compound '3P' 4-4-0 No 41066 passes Queniborough WD depot sidings on a Peterborough to Birmingham local on 22 March 1958. Depot traffic could leave the main line here and enter the depot reception sidings directly – the signal at the rear of the train carries a small shunting arm for such movements – and at the other end of the depot there was similar access. When the depot was in full operation during World War II workers arrived by passenger trains to a station built especially just inside the depot. The station area and other sidings were later used to store main-line carriages used for excursion traffic, and one stored rake is seen on the right of the picture. A large brick signalbox was built to control traffic in and out of the depot. *D. W. Webb*

Right:
Holwell Ironworks at Asfordby Hill near Melton Mowbray produced iron from the 1880s until 1962 using local ironstone, and its connection to the main line was on the Melton to Nottingham line. In 1918 the works became part of the Stanton Ironworks Co and inter-works transfers of engines occurred. From then onwards, new locomotives were mainly from Andrew Barclay, which were favoured by Stanton. Holwell's engines were always busy, and this 1959 picture of *Stanton No 36*, built in 1937, shows it shunting a wagon of molten slag. The hopper wagons of ironstone in the sidings at the lower level will have probably come from the Eaton area. *D. W. Webb*

Left:
Holwell No 15, a Hudswell Clarke engine built in 1917, is also seen at the ironworks in 1959, taking water between duties. *D. W. Webb*

Right:
Class B12/3 4-6-0 No 61533 is about to depart eastwards from Melton Mowbray with the afternoon Birmingham to Yarmouth Beach train on 11 April 1950. The engine belonged to the former M&GN depot at South Lynn and had worked the train as far as Leicester earlier in the day. The signals are set for the fast line; the left-hand signals refer to the slow line loop, which started immediately after the road bridge – this loop is still in existence as far as Brentingby. The westbound loop finishes just under the bridge. *J. M. Mason*

Below:
Beyer-Garratt 2-6-6-2 No 47967 is seen passing Saxby station on a very long Toton to Wellingborough train on 11 April 1950. This station, which closed in 1961, still sees heavy passing traffic, now destined mainly for Peterborough and the eastern counties.
J. M. Mason

Above left:
These next three pictures were taken from a Leicester London Road to Skegness day excursion in August 1958, hauled by a '4F' class 0-6-0 throughout. In the first view the train is slowing down for the junction at Saxby, with the signal 'off' for the Bourne line. The lines to and from Peterborough or Kettering via Manton pass between the platforms on the right. The well-tended station and railway were typical at the time. *D. W. Webb*

Left:
Just the other side of the road bridge, the double track became single with additional connections to the up slow and fast lines. *D. W. Webb*

Above:
In the last picture the excursion sets off to the east along the single line as the Midland main tracks turn away to the south. After the end-on junction with the M&GN at Little Bytham, the train followed that line as far as Cuckoo Junction, where it then headed north towards Boston. *D. W. Webb*

Right:
On the 13 miles from Saxby to Little Bytham, only one station was in Leicestershire – Edmondthorpe & Wymondham. In September 1954 Derby's '4F' 0-6-0 No 44031 is seen passing the station on a day excursion to Skegness. *J. M. Mason*

LEICESTER TO BURTON-UPON-TRENT LINE

Just south of the Knighton Tunnels the Midland Railway opened a line from Knighton North Junction to Desford Junction in 1849. Here it joined the route of the Leicester & Swannington Railway from Leicester West Bridge, which had opened in 1832, then continued to Coalville and eventually as far as Burton-upon-Trent. At Knighton there was a triangular junction giving access to the new line, but after the passenger trains on the branch ceased in 1964 the north-to-west curve was removed.

The opening of the new line in 1849 took some traffic off the West Bridge branch and passengers could then reach the main Midland Railway station at Campbell Street, Leicester, direct, to connect with trains to all parts of the British railway system. Despite this, some passenger trains continued to run to West Bridge until 1928 to serve Ratby and Glenfield.

In 1878 a new gas works was opened by the Aylestone Road and sidings were provided to receive the huge amount of coal that the works used. The gas works had its own small tank engines from 1885, all named after stars in the sky and planets. The last one, named *Mars II*, went into a local museum in 1970.

Towards the end of 1922 a new electricity power station was opened on the opposite side of the railway from the gas works. This too was served by the railway and in the late 1940s big improvements and extensions were made to the power station and the reception sidings. Initially, in 1922,

two 0-4-0 fireless locomotives were used to shunt in the sidings, but in 1950 these were joined by a brand new 0-4-0 steam locomotive built by Robert Stephenson & Hawthorns, and a new engine shed was built for this new arrival. In 1976 the power station closed and its rail traffic ended. All three engines have been preserved at various sites or in museums.

After crossing the River Soar on a 12-arch brick viaduct, the line passed over the former GCR main line to London. Just after this there was a short private siding into a local coal merchant's yard controlled by a ground frame inside a tiny wooden cabin. This siding was shunted daily by the westbound pick-up freight.

The only passenger station before Desford was at Kirby Muxloe, and 2 miles further on was Desford Junction, where there were extensive sidings for traffic to and from the branch line to Leicester West Bridge. On the right was the large Tubes factory, which at one time had a busy railway siding of its own for the delivery of steel and the dispatch of steel products.

Three-quarters of a mile further on was Desford station where most of the 1848 station building still survives as a private house. The gated level crossing and the signalbox were replaced by automatic barriers some years ago. Shortly after leaving Desford the railway passed through an area of much coal mining and granite quarrying before reaching Coalville. At Cliffe Hill Sidings, between Bagworth and Bardon Hill, a narrow gauge railway brought granite from Cliffe Hill quarry, 2½ miles away near Markfield; this little private railway closed in 1948.

Passenger services from Leicester to Burton-upon-Trent ceased in 1964 and Coalville Town station was closed. Coalville then became one of the largest British towns without a railway station. All the other remaining stations on the line closed at the same time, several having closed earlier. These included Bardon Hill, in 1952, though the signalbox there remains to control the level crossing and Bardon Hill granite sidings.

Until very recent times there were many busy collieries all along the whole railway from Merrylees nearly as far as Burton-upon-Trent. There were also several branch lines to collieries and a great deal of coal traffic was carried. Many of these collieries were operating throughout the period covered in this book and Coalville locomotive depot was of great importance.

Just to the east of Coalville, the Charnwood Forest Railway, which was owned by the LNWR, was crossed and there was a junction between the two lines. This railway lost its passenger trains in 1931 and ran through Whitwick and Shepshed to a small terminus at Loughborough Derby Road. Its own station at Coalville East was just before the junction, and south of there the line was owned jointly by the LNWR and the MR and ran all the way to Nuneaton through Shackerstone and Market Bosworth. Part of this route survives in preservation as 'The Battlefield Line'.

Returning to the line west of Coalville, this then passed through Ashby-de-la-Zouch and Moira before entering South Derbyshire. Just on the county boundary there was a single-track loop line through Woodville and Swadlincote, which rejoined the main route at Swadlincote Junction. This loop tapped a great deal of traffic from an area rich in brick and pipe works, based on large local deposits of suitable clay, and numerous nearby coal mines. Despite its short length the loop was not straightforward to build. There were many tight curves, steep gradients and two tunnels, Woodville (307 yards) and Midway (104 yards). Regular passenger trains on the loop ended in 1947, but until 1962 occasional holiday trains still used the line. Several pipe manufacturers and collieries had private sidings along the loop, and their own shunting engines. However, the most interesting was John Knowles (Wooden Box) Ltd, at Woodville, which had both a standard gauge line and an 18-inch gauge railway in Leicestershire with small steam locomotives to bring fireclay from its mine to the works.

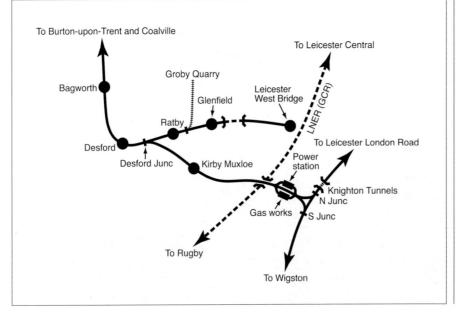

Above:
The branch line from Burton-upon-Trent joined the main line at Knighton by means of a triangle. At the North Junction direct movement was possible to and from Leicester, and at Knighton South Junction, shown in this 4 August 1962 picture, there was access to and from the south. An up Manchester Central express is passing Knighton South Junction signalbox with 'Jubilee' class No 45712 *Victory* in charge. On the left can be seen Leicester power station. *J. M. Mason*

Right:
Leicester gas works was alongside the branch line close to the bridge over the Aylestone Road. It used a series of 0-4-0 saddle tank engines from 1885 onwards, which were all named after stars in the sky or planets; the last one purchased was *Mars II*, by Robert Stephenson & Hawthorns, maker's number 7493 of 1948. They were painted red and were very well kept, as can be seen in this photograph on 30 November 1963. The Burton line is between the engine and the wagons in the background. *Mars II* was preserved initially at the Abbey Pumping Station Museum. *J. M. Mason*

Above:
A new power station was opened on Freeman's Meadow, Aylestone Road, in 1922, beside the river and on the opposite side of the branch line from the gas works. Two fireless engines came from Andrew Barclay & Sons in 1922 and 1924, No 1 and No 2, and they were powered by steam taken from the power station. Over the years the works was extended and in 1950 a new steam engine, No 3, came from Robert Stephenson & Hawthorns. A new engine shed was built solely for No 3, and both are seen here on 30 November 1963. All three engines have been preserved at different locations.
M. Mason/J. M. Mason

Below:
'Twelve Bridges' is a local name for the brick viaduct that carries the Burton branch over the River Soar. Ex-LNER Class O4/8 No 63706 is seen on a ballast train, standing on the viaduct in March 1959. The power station is behind the engine and the reception sidings are on the right, while the tall chimney on the extreme right is part of the gas works. It was most unusual to see a former LNER engine on this ex-LMS line; five more years were to pass before a link was put in between the branch and the former GCR line nearby. *J. M. Mason*

Right:
Standard '4MT' 4-6-0 No 75058 has just passed the gas works and crossed the River Soar on a Leicester to Burton-upon-Trent local in 1961. *D. W. Webb*

Left:
A Burton-upon-Trent to Leicester local train approaches the bridge over the former GCR main line, with '2P' class 4-4-0 No 40411 in charge on 18 April 1956. Behind the modern brick platelayers' hut is the siding into Billson's coal yard and a small wooden cabin for the ground frame. *M. Mason*

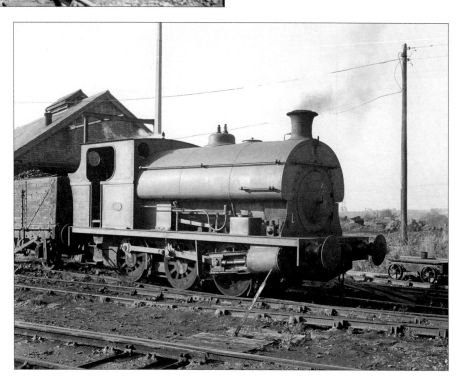

Right:
There were several collieries along the line between Desford and Coalville, all having railway sidings. Bagworth Colliery was at the end of a short branch line, and for many years two Peckett tank engines worked there. Peckett No 1404, built in 1915, is seen outside the colliery engine shed on 6 November 1965. *J. M. Mason*

Left:
Bardon Hill station closed in 1952, but when this picture of '2P' class 4-4-0 No 40682 was taken in 1956, heading a Burton to Leicester local, it was still intact. The signalbox still controls the road crossing barriers and Bardon Hill granite quarry sidings. *D. W. Webb*

Below:
On 27 May 1961 Coalville Town station was visited by the Leicester Railway Society's 21st Anniversary Special, behind 2-6-2 tank No 41321. The station closed finally in 1964 and the entire site was cleared, to leave just the two running lines. The signalbox was removed in the 1970s and the level crossing is now controlled by barriers. *M. Mason*

This page:
Around Swadlincote there were many brick and pipe works exploiting local clay. Some had their own railway sidings and one company, John Knowles (Wooden Box) Ltd, had both standard and narrow gauge tracks at Woodville, served by the Swadlincote loop line of the MR. The narrow gauge line was of only 18-inch gauge and ran from the works to the clay mines. These two pictures show *Gwen*, built by Hunslet in 1920, at the mine in 1956 and at the works in March 1958, just before the system was closed. The other engine, *Jack*, built in 1898, was almost identical. Both are preserved, *Gwen* in the USA and *Jack* in a Leeds museum. The size of the wagons was limited by the narrowness of the mine. *M. Mason*

Above:
The Leicester Railway Society Special of 27 May 1961 also visited the Charnwood Forest Railway, which ran originally to a small terminus at Loughborough Derby Road. The Special only went as far as Shepshed, where this photograph was taken. *M. Mason*

LEICESTER WEST BRIDGE TO DESFORD JUNCTION

This quiet single-track branch line lost its modest passenger service as early as 1928, then its daily goods train in 1966. Its history went back to the birth of steam railways, when George Stephenson's son Robert was the engineer responsible for its construction. The line opened in July 1832 as part of the Leicester & Swannington Railway. It had been promoted by colliery owners and local business people, principally to bring coal cheaply and easily from the Coalville area to its terminus at West Bridge, close to the heart of old Leicester. Though passengers were carried, they were not considered to be of any real value at first.

Large amounts of coal were brought down to Leicester from the western end of the new line at Swannington. Because of its situation it had been necessary to build a steep rope-worked incline of 1 in 17 to bring the loaded coal wagons for the first half-mile of their journey up from the colliery village of Swannington. Another incline was needed at Bagworth. A more difficult engineering challenge involved the building of the world's first railway tunnel at Glenfield. Though the tunnel bore

was both level and straight, it was through sand and clay, and this gave serious problems to the contractors, who had never attempted work of this magnitude before. The single-track tunnel was 1,796 yards long and was built with much narrower clearances than later tunnels. This seriously limited the dimensions of engines and rolling-stock that could pass through it, so for many years old Midland Railway 0-6-0s had sole charge of all trains.

The Leicester & Swannington Railway became part of the Midland Railway in 1847, but it was not until 1893 that a proper new passenger station was opened at West Bridge. New stations had been built at Glenfield and Ratby in 1875 and 1876, and these survived until complete closure of the line in 1966. Between Glenfield and Ratby there was a siding for Glenfield brickworks, where a private branch line set off northwards to Groby granite quarry, 1¼ miles away. This opened in 1832 but was closed in 1847 and dismantled. However, in the mid-1860s the line was reinstated and the MR put in a proper junction and sidings to handle the granite traffic. Then for nearly 100 years granite wagons were pulled along this little line, from the quarries at Groby, by small

Hunslet tank engines. In 1962 a new Fowler diesel locomotive took over the work, but its days here were short as the line closed in 1966. The diesel worked on for several more years at Croft quarry.

Both Glenfield and Ratby stations had small goods yards where local coal merchants received their supplies. At both stations there was a simple loop line commencing on the Desford side of the gated level crossing, with a single goods siding off the other end. There was no signalbox at either station, but stop signals and points were worked by levers in ground frames. Right up to the closure of the line in 1966 the daily goods trains comprised many wagons, with coal, petrol and wood being the main goods carried to Leicester.

The old 0-6-0s were replaced by Standard Class 2MT 2-6-0s for the final couple of years, as it had been found that, with a little alteration, two of these engines would pass through the narrow bore of Glenfield Tunnel. Each afternoon one would bring its train of mainly empty wagons up from West Bridge and shunt it off at Desford Junction sidings, before returning light engine to Coalville depot where both engines were based.

Above:
The new West Bridge terminus was built by the MR in 1893 to replace the 1832 station. There was a single platform with a waiting room and a loop for engines to run round their trains. Behind the buffer stop was the station office. Passenger services finished in 1928, but the extensive goods yard continued to be busy with coal, wood and petrol until the line closed in 1966. The houses on the right of this 1959 view are on Tudor Road and the largest building at the end of the station is King Richard's Road School. *D. W. Webb*

Below:
Glenfield Tunnel was 1,796 yards long, and on 27 June 1959 '2F' class 0-6-0 No 58298 emerges from its western portal. Some idea of how little clearance there was for a train can be gained from the photograph. *M. Mason*

Left:
Between Glenfield and Ratby there was a siding into Glenfield brickworks, where there was also a private branch line northwards to Groby granite quarry. The line was worked by Hunslet tank engines, and No 2, built in 1915, is seen here in May 1962 on the outskirts of Groby, where the track ran alongside the road. This line carried granite from the quarries for 100 years, and closed in 1966. *J. M. Mason*

Below:
Ratby station is pictured on 21 October 1951, when its small goods yard was still quite busy. Passenger trains had ceased in 1928, but the station was still in very good order and staffed daily. The loop line ran over the level crossing and there was a single siding for coal and goods traffic. The advertisement board was still headed LMS and usually carried posters. There was a ground frame to work the two Home signals and the points. Six red fire buckets hung on brackets outside the gents, below the sign over its entrance. *J. M. Mason*

Above:
On 3 May 1958 the daily goods from West Bridge is at New Bridge level crossing, where Desford Lane from Ratby village was crossed. The crossing-keeper has just closed the gates in case any road traffic comes along. The brick hut is extremely old and probably dates back to the line's early days. Midland '2F' 0-6-0 No 58298 is taking its train of empties as far as Desford Junction Sidings. *M. Mason*

Below:
Having just crossed New Bridge crossing, No 58298 is passing the fixed Distant signal before Desford Junction on the same day. This section ran beside the Kirby Muxloe to Desford Road, and crossed the road at another gated level crossing just before the junction. *M. Mason*

WIGSTON TO RUGBY LINE

In July 1840 the Midland Counties Railway (MCR) opened a line from Leicester to Rugby, where its trains connected with those of the London & Birmingham Railway. This enabled Leicester people to reach the capital directly by railway for the first time, in around 5½ hours. To the north of Leicester the MCR went as far as Nottingham and Derby. At Derby it joined the North Midland Railway, and its timetables showed connections from Hull, York, Leeds and Sheffield. So, as early as 1840, the Leicester to Rugby railway line was very important in the railway network as a carrier of passengers and freight. All trains were described as 'mixed'.

In June 1844 the MCR became part of the Midland Railway, and in 1857 the Midland opened its new line to Hitchin. Midland trains could then reach London at the GNR terminus at King's Cross, until the MR's own terminus at St Pancras was opened. In 1864 a new direct route to Birmingham from Leicester via Nuneaton was opened. These developments reduced the importance of the Rugby line, which then became a secondary route between Wigston and Rugby, through a purely rural landscape, for nearly 98 years until its complete closure at the end of 1961.

Right up to the end the line carried a surprising number of through freight trains. The local passenger trains were well used and called at all five stations between Leicester and Rugby. Four of these, at South Wigston, Countesthorpe, Broughton Astley and Ullesthorpe, had staggered platforms. Only the tiny Leire Halt was unstaffed and had very basic shelters on its two platforms; it had no signalbox, sidings or signals. At South Wigston and Countesthorpe, the stations were in the centre of the villages and were at level crossings. There was also a level crossing where the Watling Street A5 trunk road crossed the line at Willey Crossing, just over 5 miles from Rugby. The small Midland Railway box here, with its two Home and two Distant signals, saw both excitement and tragedy from time to time, when road vehicles crashed into the heavy level crossing gates. On at least one occasion a driver was killed by a train after a vehicle had crashed through the gates.

For a time after traffic on the Rugby line had ceased the short section between Wigston North Junction and Wigston Central Junction remained open for freight trains to be diverted back round to rejoin the Nuneaton line at Glen Parva.

Below:
The Rugby line left the Midland main line at Wigston North Junction. LMS 'Crab' 2-6-0 No 42783 is seen at the junction on 26 April 1958, the signals indicating that the goods train is about to take the Rugby line. *M. Mason*

Right:
The platforms at South Wigston station were staggered on either side of the level crossing. A local train from Leicester to Rugby, hauled by a 2-6-4 tank, is passing the former Midland signalbox on a misty morning on 9 December 1961. In just three weeks the line will be closed. *D. W. Webb*

Below:
Two small children and their grandfather watch a train from Rugby run into South Wigston station behind 2-6-4 tank No 42062 on the same day. This was the only station on the line where a footbridge could be used when the level crossing gates were closed. *D. W. Webb*

Left:
Countesthorpe station, which was in the heart of the village, was kept beautifully and used well. On Saturday 25 March 1961 an ex-LNWR 0-8-0 is seen on a southbound freight just before going over the level crossing and past the up platform. *D. W. Webb*

Right:
It's mid-morning on the same day, and passengers are waiting to board a Leicester train at Broughton Astley. Rugby's Class 4P 2-6-4 tank No 42062 is in charge. *D. W. Webb*

Left:
Stanier '8F' 2-8-0 No 48603 of Willesden depot charges through the tiny unstaffed Leire Halt with a long coal train to London on the same day. *D. W. Webb*

Right:
Ullesthorpe station was nearly 8 miles from Rugby. This picture, also taken on 25 March 1961, shows the staggered platforms, which were joined by a boarded foot crossing. The station house and the single-storey station building were on the Leicester platform, and there was a small wooden waiting room on the Rugby side. *D. W. Webb*

Below:
Leicester's '4F' class 0-6-0 No 44182 shunts in Ullesthorpe goods yard on the same day. The remainder of its train stands on the up line in the foreground. *D. W. Webb*

WIGSTON TO HINCKLEY AND NUNEATON

There was no direct line between Leicester and Birmingham until the mid-1860s. When opened, the new line gave the important town of Hinckley a direct route to both places and also to the LNWR West Coast main line at Nuneaton. At its height the line carried a great deal of granite from quarries along its route and there was also a 2-mile line northwards from Narborough to Enderby to tap this important traffic. The Enderby branch was owned jointly by the MR and LNWR and also carried the granite from other quarries in the Huncote and Narborough areas. During World War II, trains of petrol wagons stood for some time on the branch and old LMS passenger coaches were also stored there. No doubt these were connected with the war effort.

Between Croft and Elmesthorpe stations a private branch line of half a mile ran south to Stoney Stanton granite quarries. There were several sidings by the main line and a signalbox, which was normally switched out with all signals at clear unless there was quarry traffic. Opposite the sidings was another siding, which served a concrete pipe works and a narrow gauge tramway. This ran northwards for about half a mile to Earl Shilton granite quarries. At one time several narrow gauge steam engines worked there.

While all the granite quarries mentioned here have been closed for several years and

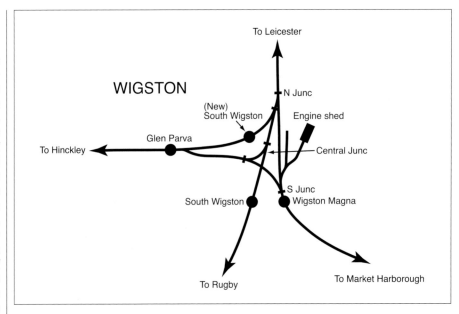

WIGSTON

To Leicester

N Junc

(New) South Wigston

Engine shed

Glen Parva

To Hinckley

Central Junc

S Junc
Wigston Magna

South Wigston

To Rugby

To Market Harborough

the Enderby line has gone, there is still a very active quarry at Croft. This has been modernised and extended over the years, and retains its rail connection. Regular trains leave Croft Sidings daily taking Croft granite and concrete products.

Though all the passenger stations between Leicester London Road and Hinckley were closed in 1968, public demand has seen Narborough station re-open and a new station provided at South Wigston. However, Blaby, with its wooden platforms and buildings on the embankment, Croft and Elmesthorpe stations appear to have gone for ever. Hinckley is a busy commuter station, but

its extensive goods yard and large goods shed have been swept away.

Despite the loss of all its local freight services and some of its intermediate stations, the line is still a busy through route for both passenger and goods traffic.

Another important line linked Wigston South Junction and Wigston Glen Parva on the Birmingham line. This was principally for freight traffic, but when the main line south of Nuneaton was closed for any reason, expresses could be sent along the branch to Wigston. They used this south curve to Wigston South Junction before heading south, prior to regaining their route to Euston via Market Harborough and Northampton.

Left:
The line to Birmingham New Street via Hinckley and Nuneaton left the Midland main line at Wigston North Junction. Stanier '3P' 2-6-2 tank No 145, still in LMS condition, is seen there hauling a Birmingham express on 14 May 1948. *J. M. Mason*

Above right:
A local passenger train to Birmingham passes under the former GCR main line near Whetstone having just left Blaby station. The locomotive, '4MT' 2-6-0 No 43003, was one of the early members of its class, and on 25 September 1954 still carries its original double chimney. *M. Mason*

Right:
An afternoon freight train from Leicester to Nuneaton passes Croft station hauled by 'Patriot' class No 45537 *Private E. Sykes VC* on 20 May 1961. The station was used quite heavily by commuters to Leicester and Hinckley, but closed in 1968. *M. Mason*

MARKET HARBOROUGH TO RUGBY LINE

West of Market Harborough the LNWR line from Peterborough to Rugby ran along the southern tip of Leicestershire for several miles. The countryside was purely agricultural and the railway passed through some very pleasant villages. The first station was at Lubenham, then followed Theddingworth, Welford & Kilworth, Yelvertoft (in Northamptonshire) and finally Lilbourne. All these stations showed their LNWR origins to the end, with buildings and signalling lasting well. However, during the 1950s the signalbox at Theddingworth was burned down and was rebuilt as a flat-roofed cabin on the original brick base. Local traffic on the line was very light in its final years and few trains stopped at all its stations, where there was often only a porter/signalman in sole charge.

The loss of the direct route from Leicester London Road to Rugby allowed passengers to travel to Rugby via either Nuneaton Trent Valley or Market Harborough. This gave enthusiasts the opportunity to enjoy a pleasant circular journey on a summer's evening, taking in the Rugby to Market Harborough line before it was axed in 1966.

Left:
There were six stations between Market Harborough and Rugby on this ex-LNWR country branch line from Peterborough. The first was at Lubenham, which is seen in late 1960 complete with its LNWR buildings and unmanned signalbox. The line closed in 1966. *D. W. Webb*

Left:
The second station served Theddingworth, which was half a mile from the village and was staffed by a porter/signalman. The level crossing gates were operated by a large hand wheel, which can be seen through the signalbox window in this late-1960 view. Some years earlier, the top half of the signalbox had been destroyed by fire and was rebuilt with a flat roof. The tall LNWR signal is being passed at speed by Standard '5MT' No 73024 on a Peterborough to Rugby train that did not call here. *D. W. Webb*

3. THE GN&LNWR JOINT LINE

Another substantial railway line, serving Melton Mowbray, passed north to south through rural eastern Leicestershire. This was built, during a time of great optimism, jointly by the Great Northern Railway (GNR) and the London & North Western Railway (LNWR), and was opened as a through route in 1879. The GNR line to Leicester Belgrave Road, opened in 1882 for goods and for passengers on 1 January 1883, left the Joint line at Marefield.

The line ran between Saxondale Junction and Bottesford Junctions in the north to the LNWR near Market Harborough in the south. From Melton Mowbray southwards the buildings and equipment were of LNWR design, and north of there they were GNR; the Belgrave Road branch was pure GNR. At the north end of Melton Mowbray station, which was renamed Melton Mowbray North in 1950, there was a large LNWR signalbox on stilts, which was said to sway in strong winds.

Extensive deposits of ironstone were found during the excavation of the deep cutting south of Tilton station, and quarrying began here on the west side of the railway a few years later. Until around 1929 horses were used in the quarries, after which a 3-foot gauge railway using steam locomotives brought from other local quarries replaced the horses. Ironstone was tipped from the narrow-gauge wagons into main-line wagons on a siding in the goods yard just north of

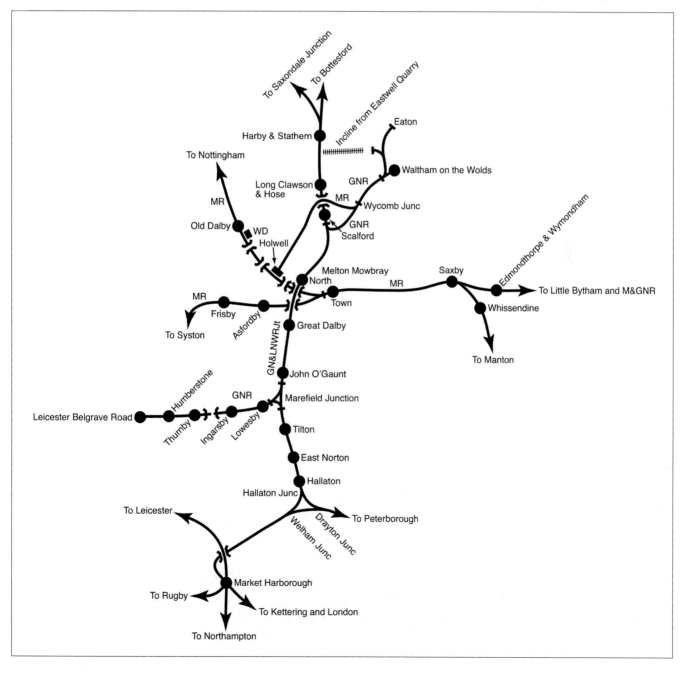

Tilton station. After World War II the Stanton company replaced all its narrow gauge quarry systems with motor lorries. The Tilton system survived until 1950, when it was the last of the company's 3-foot gauge systems still operating. The new lorries were kept in the old engine shed and ran to and from a new quarry on the east side of the railway via a new bridge over the line. A new tipping chute was built so that the lorries could tip ironstone directly into railway wagons below. The quarries closed in 1961, and ironstone traffic from Tilton finished after more than 70 years.

Other substantial amounts of ironstone were found north-east of Melton Mowbray, and a small network of single-track lines was built from Holwell and Scalford to Eaton, mainly to carry ironstone. At Wycomb Junction the former MR line from Holwell joined the GNR Scalford to Eaton line. Just over 2 miles further on towards Eaton, a small station was built by the GNR at Waltham on the Wolds. This had a single platform, a modest goods yard and goods shed. A large station master's house and a short row of houses for other GNR employees were built. While there was never a regular passenger service, the station was extremely busy before the 1914 war, with hunting and local racing traffic,

involving both passengers and horses. Agricultural, general freight and coal traffic was also dealt with. The line to Waltham had opened in 1883 and was extended to Eaton a year later as more ironstone was found and quarries were opened there. Waltham station was then on a short spur from the line to Eaton and a GNR signalbox was built. The only other signalbox on these lines was at Wycomb Junction.

At Eaton there was an array of sidings next to a tipping dock where a metre-gauge steam-hauled railway brought ironstone from the quarries. The MR line from Wycomb Junction to Holwell did not open until 1887 and could then take ironstone direct from the Eaton area to Holwell Ironworks near Asfordby.

Between Waltham on the Wolds station and Eaton, one further short line was built by the GNR with the intention of serving Eastwell quarries. However, it was never used as the output went the opposite way down a cable-worked double incline to Stathern Ironstone Sidings on the GN&LNWR Joint line. This unused branch was taken up and the ironstone company used the route when extending its own 3-foot gauge system towards Branston. A road bridge built by the GNR over this line survives to this day.

South of Melton Mowbray the station at John O'Gaunt was next to a large dairy, from which milk was regularly dispatched by rail. The station at East Norton was a little way from the village and was just north of East Norton Tunnel (444 yards). Hallaton was the final station before Welham Junction, where the LNWR line from Peterborough was joined. It was then only 3 miles to Market Harborough. Prior to World War I there was a curve from Hallaton Junction, a little south of the station, through Medbourne to Drayton Junction on the LNWR line; this enabled trains from Leicester Belgrave Road to reach Peterborough direct, also using a west-to-south curve at Marefield.

Of the stations south of Melton Mowbray North, Great Dalby and Tilton closed in 1953, and John O'Gaunt, East Norton and Hallaton in 1957; Melton Mowbray North itself and stations north thereof closed in 1953. There was an 832-yard tunnel at Hose, between Scalford and Long Clawson & Hose station. Closure south of Marefield Junction came in 1963 and north of there in 1964. Throughout its life the line carried heavy coal trains from Nottinghamshire to the south, while in its last years East Coast holiday trains from Leicester Belgrave Road were the only regular passenger trains.

Far left:
A Joint line warning sign against trespassers near Melton Mowbray North station, photographed in 1962. *D. W. Webb*

Left:
The LNWR signalbox at Melton Mowbray North station, seen from a Leicester Belgrave Road to Mablethorpe train in September 1961. This structure was said to rock in high winds. From here southwards, buildings and equipment were of LNWR design, and northwards of GNR design. *D. W. Webb*

Above:
John O'Gaunt station is seen looking south from the road bridge in 1959. The dairy sidings provided regular traffic for the railway and local coal merchants used the goods yard. However, the area was purely farming country and passengers were few, even before the days of competition from road transport. The last public passenger trains had called here two years earlier, but the LMS station name boards are still in place on both platforms and the station is in good order. All signals are 'off' and the LNWR signalbox, just off the end of the up platform, is switched out. There is a 14-arch brick viaduct just around the bend south of the station. *D. W. Webb*

Right:
A returning Skegness to Leicester Belgrave Road holiday train is turning on to the GNR Leicester line at Marefield Junction on 5 August 1961. The GN&LNWR Joint line to the south passes behind the signalbox. This was originally Marefield North Junction in the days when there was a triangular junction here. *J. M. Mason*

Above:
Colwick-based Austerity 2-8-0 No 90215 is on
an up freight approaching Marefield Junction on
22 June 1959. Even after local passenger
services ceased in 1957, there was still heavy
coal traffic on the Joint line for some years.
J. M. Mason

Left:
Tilton-on-the-Hill station was to the east of the
village down in a valley. Considerable deposits
of ironstone were revealed when the cutting
south of the station was excavated, and this was
quarried until 1961. The ironstone was taken by
rail from the goods yard, where a new chute
allowed the lorries, which had replaced the old
narrow-gauge quarry railway in 1950, to tip the
ore straight into wagons below. This picture
shows Class J11/3 0-6-0 No 64354 passing
Tilton station on 13 October 1962 with a
special. By then all signals were left at clear
unless the signalbox was open. *J. M. Mason*

Right:
Empty coal wagons from Thurnby and Humberstone goods yards, hauled by a Class J39 0-6-0, pass over the gated level crossing at Forest Road on 6 May 1959. The footbridge was later removed as it was in a poor state and was unnecessary, with so few trains on the line. The Distant arm on the concrete-posted signal is Leicester Passenger's fixed down Distant. *D. W. Webb*

Below:
A Mablethorpe day excursion passes the level crossing and tiny GNR signalbox at Forest Road on 23 July 1961. *J. M. Mason*

Colwick 'B1' No 61163 approaches Humberstone station in 1960 with a day excursion to the East Coast. There is a GNR notice board in front of the GNR signal on the left. *D. W. Webb*

Below:
In this general view of Humberstone station from the signalbox steps, Class B1 No 61092 is running in and a fair number of day trippers to the seaside are waiting to join the train. *D. W. Webb*

Right:
Class B1 No 61281 is climbing up to Thurnby & Scraptoft station, passing the signalbox and goods yard. All the signalling here, including ground signals, was of GNR origin. *D. W. Webb*

Below:
This short wooden-posted GNR Home signal was the down starter for Thurnby & Scraptoft station and lasted until the line closed in June 1964. It was photographed in June 1962, when the tracks were already becoming overgrown by weeds. Excursion trains finished that September. *D. W. Webb*

Below right:
Class B1 4-6-0 No 61177 is about to cross the bridge over Station Road, Thurnby, on 27 July 1958 after stopping at the station. A large housing estate had been built close to the station and this boosted passenger numbers on these summer seaside trains. The length of the train can clearly be seen. *D. W. Webb*

Above:
With the withdrawal of older engines, the daily goods train from Colwick was taken over by Ivatt '4MT' 2-6-0s. The returning train, hauled by No 43152, emerges from the eastern end of Thurnby Tunnel (516 yards) on a Saturday afternoon in the early 1960s. *D. W. Webb*

Left:
After withdrawal of local passenger services and workers' trains, the stations on the branch remained intact for some years. This GNR name board on the platform at Ingarsby and those on the signalbox were still in good order in 1961. *D. W. Webb*

PASSENGER SERVICES ON THE EX-GCR MAIN LINE

All the passenger stations in Leicestershire on the former GCR line were built as island platforms, including Leicester Central and Loughborough. Belgrave & Birstall had no sidings and catered only for passengers. Loop lines were provided at some stations to relieve the possible delays to passenger trains by slower mineral trains, as the line was basically a double-track main-line railway. South of Leicester Central station the up and down loop lines were extended, and during the last war a new connection was put in from the down main line to the down loop just south of Marlow Road bridge. This meant that goods trains could enter the loop from the south more directly.

In the 1940s the former GCR passenger engines were gradually displaced by the newly introduced 'B1' class 4-6-0s on most of the express and local services. This was seen plainly by the public, since green 'B1s' now headed their trains of varnished teak carriages instead of the usual black engines. Despite Nationalisation of the railways in January 1948, the green liveries lasted for several more years, generally until the engines went away to the works for overhaul.

Similarly, the carriages lost their varnished teak splendour when they were repainted in the new standard crimson and cream of BR. In 1946 the LNER had made strenuous efforts to replace many of its old main-line carriages with modern steel-panelled ones, painted in ersatz teak livery to match existing teak stock. At first these new coaches were only used on the East Coast main line from King's Cross and few reached the line through Leicester Central. However, when 'The South Yorkshireman' express was introduced it was made up of the new coaches and was very impressive.

From their introduction in 1936 Class V2 2-6-2s worked regularly through Leicester on all types of trains, and were still to be seen occasionally in the last few months before September 1966. In 1949 six Class A3 4-6-2s arrived at Leicester Central shed and three more went to Neasden. These more powerful engines took over most of the express passenger trains between London Marylebone and Manchester London Road from the 'B1s', which were hard pressed to keep time on occasions. The 'A3s' were part of the Leicester scene for the next eight years and at one time included the famous *Flying Scotsman*. Eventually they were transferred back to the East Coast main line by the end of 1957.

Quite a variety of types of engines worked the local trains, including 'B17' and 'B1' 4-6-0s, 'K3' and 'K2' 2-6-0s, 'J39', 'J11' and 'J6' 0-6-0s, and the new 'L1' 2-6-4 tanks. Some local trains from Sheffield Victoria and Nottingham Victoria terminated at Leicester Central, and after using the turntable by Great Central Street their engines returned north on their trains.

In the late 1940s it was still possible to see old GCR 4-6-0s working through Leicester, especially on Cup Final specials to Wembley. Class D11 4-4-0s worked fairly regularly from Sheffield Victoria and Nottingham as far south as Leicester Central station even in 1959. One of the last was *Prince Albert* from Staveley, which in 1958 came in every evening for several weeks on the same train.

Below:
After World War II ex-GCR 'Director' class 4-4-0s were seen infrequently at Leicester. However, at the end of the 1950s an evening train to Leicester was hauled by one from Staveley shed. No 62663 *Prince Albert* is seen on this train at Abbey Lane Sidings, just north of Leicester Central, on 11 July 1958. *M. Mason*

Left:
Normally all through passenger trains changed their engines at Leicester Central – the fresh engine stood in one of the bay platforms at the south end of the station or in a siding at the north end. 'Royal Scot' 4-6-0 No 46106 *Gordon Highlander* waits in the south bay on 16 May 1962; this engine was fitted experimentally with BR-type smoke deflectors. *M. Mason*

Right:
One of the original Class K3 2-6-0s, No 61804, built in 1920 by the GNR, is about to run on to the turntable at Leicester after bringing in a local train from Nottingham in August 1959. *J. M. Mason*

Left:
Green-liveried Class 'B1' No 61313 leaves Leicester Central on a Sunday Sheffield Victoria to Swindon express on 6 November 1949. The engine is from Sheffield Darnall depot and has not been changed at Leicester. There are two GCR lower-quadrant signals in the picture, and the left-hand one has a concrete post. There was an identical water tank to the one on the left hidden behind the engine. *J. M. Mason*

Above:
Light engines used the goods loop lines from the engine shed at Leicester South Goods to travel to and from the Central station. Standard Class 5MT 4-6-0 No 73053 has just been uncoupled from 'The South Yorkshireman' and is immediately running forward to the shed. A few minutes later the express, with the fresh engine, will follow on the main line to London Marylebone. On the left of the picture another light engine is just about to leave the down loop on its way to the station. *D. W. Webb*

Right:
A Sunday morning express to Marylebone passes Leicester South Goods junction on 27 July 1958 behind Class B1 No 61085. This was the first locomotive of its class to be withdrawn from normal service, in November 1961. *D. W. Webb*

Left:
An up morning express to Marylebone climbs away from Leicester towards Aylestone behind Class V2 2-6-2 No 60842 on Sunday 27 July 1958. *D. W. Webb*

Right:
The up 'Master Cutler' is approaching Aylestone in August 1958, passing under one of the many brick overbridges on the line. Class V2 2-6-2 No 60842 was at Leicester depot for some years. *D. W. Webb*

Left:
Class J11 0-6-0 No 64330 heads a long local passenger train away from Leicester on its way to Rugby Central on 3 June 1954. *M. Mason*

Above:
After heavy snow on a cold February morning in 1955, Class B1 No 61201 is near Whetstone with an up local train. *M. Mason*

Below:
An up express to Marylebone nears Ashby Magna station behind Class V2 2-6-2 No 60871 on 3 September 1955. The outside tracks are the goods loops, which started just past the rear of the train. Many of the coaches are ex-LNER and all are in crimson and cream livery. A few years later the M1 motorway was built parallel to the railway, a few yards over the hedge on the right. *M. Mason*

Above:
Ashby Magna station is neat and tidy as ex-GWR 4-6-0 No 6906 *Chicheley Hall* speeds through on the Bournemouth to York express on 16 June 1962. The down goods loop commenced immediately outside the tunnel, which is behind the signalbox on the right. The tall lattice-posted Home signal has co-acting arms because of the road bridge at the north end of the station. The first coach is a Thompson seven-compartment Corridor 3rd, while the rest of the train is Standard Mark 1 stock. Work on the construction of the M1 motorway started a few months later on the left of the railway. *J. M. Mason*

Left:
Class A3 Pacific No 60090 *Grand Parade* worked from Leicester Central shed from February to May 1949. After returning to the East Coast main line it went to Scotland permanently in 1950. Still with the previous allocation 'New England' on its buffer beam and in LNER green, *Grand Parade* nears Ashby Magna with an up excursion on 15 May 1949; all the coaches are in LNER teak livery. *J. M. Mason*

EX-LNER LINES IN LEICESTERSHIRE

79

FREIGHT SERVICES ON THE EX-GCR MAIN LINE

From the very start the GCR line through Leicestershire carried a great deal of coal and steel products from the North to the South, and right up to its final year of operation in 1966 heavy coal trains continued to run non-stop from Annesley to Woodford Halse. Express fish trains from Grimsby were also seen daily until the final years and were hauled principally by Class K3 2-6-0s during our period. Very occasionally, in the 1940s, ex-GCR engines pulled these trains.

During World War II USA-built 2-8-0 engines were seen frequently on the line on military and ordinary goods trains, prior to being sent overseas after the invasion. Many British-built 'Austerity' 2-8-0s were also used. After the war the LNER bought 200 'Austerity' engines and these worked through Leicester Central as well as many still owned by the Ministry of Supply. However, most heavy goods trains were still hauled by ex-GCR Class O4s, some of which had been rebuilt when they had needed major repairs.

By 1950 ex-GCR 4-6-0s were seen rarely, but early in that year Class 'B7' No 61711 was observed as it laboured slowly southwards, up the long gradient through Aylestone, on a heavy coal train – work for which it was quite unsuitable.

In 1949 several of the rebuilt Class O4s, as Class O1, were moved to Annesley depot to work fast freights through Leicester, and by 1950 a total of 51 were at Annesley. This became one of the fastest unfitted freight services in Britain, mainly comprising coal trains and the returning empties. A few years later, brand new Class 9F 2-10-0s took over from the 'O1s' and stayed on this work until 1965, when through freight services ceased.

In Leicestershire, the only industry having a direct outlet to the line was Mountsorrel Granite, whose private railway line fed important traffic to Swithland Sidings until the early 1950s.

Local daily pick-up goods trains were in the hands of older 0-6-0s, and in the late 1940s and early 1950s two Class J5 0-6-0s did this work. Only one tank engine was needed to shunt the Braunstone Gate goods depot and the yard at Leicester South Goods, and this often spent several hours standing by the signalbox between spells of work. The engines involved during our period, in order, were Class J69 No 68491, 'J50' No 68981, 'J52' No 68839 and ex-LMS No 47203, prior to the arrival of a 300hp diesel in the early 1960s.

Below:
Stanier LMS '3P' 2-6-2 tank No 40165 went to Leicester Central after the line became part of the LMR. It worked locally, including trips to Abbey Lane Sidings, where it is seen shunting on 4 July 1959. The main lines are in front of the fine GCR signalbox in the background. This box was normally open only when the sidings were being shunted; at other times all signals were at clear. Traffic into the sidings was coal and petrol. *J. M. Mason*

Above:
An up Annesley to Woodford mixed freight is entering the up goods loop at Leicester Central station on 14 April 1951. Class O1 2-8-0 No 63865 has just crossed the Northgate Street bridge at the head of its immense train. *J. M. Mason*

Left:
At the south end of Leicester Central station on 14 June 1962 Class O4/8 2-8-0 No 63720 is on an up freight. By this time these engines were rare as far south as Leicester. *J. M. Mason*

Above:
This view of Braunstone Gate goods yard in the summer of 1961 is from Upperton Road bridge. From the left can be seen the carriage sheds, Leicester North Goods signalbox, the goods warehouse and coal yard, and the hydraulic house between the spires of St Mary de Castro church and the Cathedral. The River Soar passes under the bridges in the foreground – the left-hand bridge carries the main and loop lines. Leicester North Goods signalbox's down Home signal has co-acting arms. *D. W. Webb*

Above:
Most shunting in Leicester goods yard was done by 0-6-0 tank engines, but here Class N5 0-6-2 tank No 69360 is on that duty on 15 April 1954. The brake-van was coupled to the engine for the use of the yard shunters. Leicester power station is seen in the background. *M. Mason*

Right:
Class V2 2-6-2 No 60853 has just taken water in the up goods loop and sets off again with an up freight on 22 April 1951. The fast lines are on the left of the train and the line in the foreground is a shunting line between the goods yard and sidings at Leicester South Goods. Upperton Road viaduct is in the background. *J. M. Mason*

Immingham shed's 'K3' class 2-6-0 No 61939 heads an up fish train past Leicester South Goods on 13 June 1962. *J. M. Mason*

Below:
An Annesley to Woodford Halse fast goods has just passed under the bridge carrying the line to Burton-upon-Trent on 18 April 1964. The engine, Class 9F 2-10-0 No 92021, was built originally with a Crosti boiler, but altered after a few years. Of the tracks in the foreground the nearer is the long siding and the other is the down goods loop. This train faces a continuous gradient for around 10 miles to the other side of Ashby Magna. *M. Mason*

Right:
Class 9F 2-10-0 No 92009 passes the start of Leicester South Goods down goods loop with an up freight on 16 May 1964. There was a sand drag at the end of the loop to trap any runaways. A complete train of empty wagons, with brake-van, occupies the long siding on the right. Even at this late time in the line's decline, frequent long goods trains were still operating. *J. M. Mason*

Below:
An up afternoon fish train approaches Aylestone, on the outskirts of Leicester, on 3 June 1954. Ex-GWR 'Hall' class No 6979 *Helperly Hall* had earlier brought the down Bournemouth to York express from Banbury to Leicester, and is returning home on this fish train. *M. Mason*

Above:
ROD Class O4/3 2-8-0 No 63862 has just crossed over the Wigston to Rugby line with an up coal train on 7 May 1949. The parapet of the bridge over the branch line can be seen on the left of the train, which is travelling slowly on the long gradient. *J. M. Mason*

Left:
Class O4/3 2-8-0 No 63713 bursts from under a road bridge with an up loose-coupled coal train as it climbs towards Ashby Magna on 25 March 1950. *J. M. Mason*

Above:
On 18 May 1963 Ashby Magna signalbox is passed by a fully fitted van train, hauled by '9F' 2-10-0 No 92076. The entrance to Ashby Tunnel in the left background is hidden by a coal wagon. *M. Mason*

Right:
An up train of flat wagons carrying steel is nearing Ashby Magna on 2 July 1959 behind '9F' 2-10-0 No 92030 with steam to spare. The first wagon is a single bolster, in use because of the overhanging load on the second wagon. *J. M. Mason*

LEICESTER CENTRAL LOCOMOTIVE SHED

The main purpose of Leicester depot (38C/15E) was to provide locomotives for the passenger services on the line, though there was some local freight work. Since most express passenger trains changed engines at Leicester Central, there was a lot of light engine running between the station and the depot. These engines took the loop lines from Leicester North Goods to the depot, except on Sundays when North Goods box was closed. Only about 23 engines were allocated to the depot, which closed in July 1964. Because of this there was no mechanical coaling plant and the original 1899 coaling stage remained in use. Full wagons of coal were run up the steep incline to the stage and past the chute, then were run back singly as required. It was always a fine sight to see the yard shunting engine charging a group of loaded 'loco coal' wagons up the steep slope.

Left:
The completion of the dieselisation of the railways in East Anglia in September 1962 caused the remaining locomotives there to be transferred to other parts of British Railways. On 28 February 1959 Class B1 4-6-0 No 61008 *Kudu* stands outside the front of the four-road Leicester Central shed, having left Stratford depot (30A) in East London as part of the changes a few years earlier. The tender on the left is attached to a Class V2 2-6-2. *D. W. Webb*

Below:
Class A3 4-6-2 No 60111 *Enterprise* is outside Leicester shed in June 1955. The engine went to Neasden depot at the London end of the line in February 1949 in full LNER green livery as No 111, with LNER on its tender. It was transferred to Leicester in early 1955 and stayed until September 1957. *D. W. Webb*

Right:
Tank locomotives were not seen often at Leicester Central, until the arrival in the late 1950s of modern Class L1 2-6-4 tanks. One solitary ex-GCR Class A5 4-6-2 tank, No 69800 of 1911, worked from Leicester shed for a time and is seen there on 27 October 1957. *D. W. Webb*

Left:
'Royal Scot' 4-6-0 No 46118 *Royal Welch Fusilier* stands at Leicester Central shed. Several of these engines spent their final years on the former GCR line after being displaced by diesels on the West Coast main line. The start of the long slope up to the coaling stage is on the left, in front of one of Leicester's stored 'V2s'. Each pair of the four tracks into the shed was served by a water column, with the main water tank above the coaling stage. The main lines ran in the far background, in front of the houses. *J. M. Mason*

Right:
Locomotives from Woodford Halse or Neasden often spent a while at Leicester depot *en route* to or from works visits. Ex-GCR Class J10 No 65158 was there on 5 May 1960, when on its way to Gorton Works from Woodford Halse for scrapping. *M. Mason*

5. RUTLAND

England's smallest county had perhaps more than its fair share of railway activity, but of its 13 stations only one survives in use today, at Oakham. Virtually all Rutland's lines were owned by the LMS, though there was a short piece of the LNER (ex-GNR) just inside the county at Essendine and Ryhall. The busiest section of line in Rutland was, and still is, part of the Syston to Peterborough railway, which opened in 1848. This line carries heavy traffic, being the main route from the Midlands to East Anglia.

At Manton the line to Kettering continues south for 16 miles and the line to Stamford and Peterborough turns to the east. It took from 1875 to 1880 to build the Kettering line, which was through difficult country and included the massive Welland Viaduct at Harringworth. There were four tunnels between Oakham and Harringworth, at Manton (746 yards), Wing (352 yards), Glaston (1846 yards) and Seaton (208 yards). The viaduct over the River Welland is undoubtedly the principal engineering feature of the railways in Rutland and, at 1,286 yards long with 82 arches, is an impressive structure. It took more than two years to build and its 16 million bricks were all manufactured on site.

Despite its small size, Rutland boasts two busy market towns, Oakham and Uppingham. The latter was served by a short single-track branch line from Seaton, on the former LNWR line from Market Harborough to Peterborough. The Uppingham branch was 3½ miles long, opened in 1894 and closed completely in 1964. For many years special trains were run to and from London Euston to carry pupils of Uppingham School at the beginning and end of each term.

There was another single-track route from Seaton, which connected with the Syston to Peterborough line at Luffenham, with a small intermediate station at Morcott. This short line had been opened in June 1850 by the LNWR as part of its Rugby to Stamford and Peterborough route. It was built originally with double track and involved a 448-yard tunnel at Morcott. Construction of the Seaton to South Luffenham section began in 1846 and was not finished until 1850. From the start the LNWR was dependent on the Midland Railway to allow its trains to reach the important town of Peterborough.

Subsequently, to avoid any potential problem, in 1859 the LNWR built an extension from Seaton as far as Yarwell Junction on its Northampton to Peterborough line. Consequently the Seaton to South Luffenham line via Morcott immediately lost its main-line importance and in due course was singled to become a mere country branch line.

From Seaton, both the Uppingham branch trains and those to Stamford via Morcott were worked on a push-and-pull basis for many years. They used the same bay platform at Seaton and two parallel tracks ran from the station for some distance before dividing. Towards the end of normal services the Uppingham branch was worked conventionally with the branch engine running round its single carriage at both ends of each trip.

There was a small engine shed at Seaton, which was a sub-shed of Rugby's LNWR depot. Until the early 1950s veteran LNWR 2-4-2 tanks were used, but these were replaced on the Uppingham service by a new Ivatt 2-6-2 tank, No 41278. Various other engines were used in the 1950s including ex-GNR 'C12' 4-4-2 tanks, LMS 4-4-2 tank No 41949, and an LMS '3F' tank. In its last years ex-LMS 4-4-2 tank No 41975, which had come from the old London, Tilbury & Southend Section, worked the line.

In 1966 all remaining ex-LNWR lines through Rutland were closed and the once busy junctions at Seaton were no more. Happily, the station buildings at Seaton remain and are maintained very well, a credit to their present owners. North of Oakham one quadruple-track section remains in use, though the slow mineral trains of steam days are around no longer to hinder impatient passenger trains.

Rutland once saw much industrial activity. In particular there was extensive quarrying for ironstone, especially around Cottesmore, Burley and Exton, just east of Oakham. In 1882 the Midland Railway opened a 2-mile branch line from near Ashwell station to Cottesmore to carry ironstone trains from the Cottesmore mines. In due course quarries opened at Burley and Exton Park, both connected to the Cottesmore branch. The Cottesmore mines system was built to 3-foot gauge and the others to standard gauge. Cottesmore was the first to close, in 1957, and Burley

lasted until 1962, while the very extensive Exton Park system, which had opened as late as 1951, lasted only until 1973. There were two other long-lived ironstone quarries at Market Overton and Pilton, with their own railway systems, but in common with all British ironstone mines they too closed completely when a decision was made, in the early 1970s, to import higher-grade iron ore in future.

There had been a modest ironstone quarry at Uppingham, which was connected to the LNWR (later LMS) branch line, but it had a short life and closed in 1926. Its small tank engines saw service at other quarries and one, a Peckett named *Uppingham*, is preserved locally at the Rutland Railway Museum, near Cottesmore.

In 1928 a cement works was opened at Ketton, to use an abundance of local stone. The factory prospered and still produces a large amount of cement. A short line to the works was built by the company just to the east of Ketton & Collyweston station. Some cement still leaves the works by rail, and coal, used in the manufacturing process, comes in that way.

At Essendine, a short piece of the GNR/LNER East Coast main line passes through a corner of Rutland. There was once a comparatively large junction station here, for such a relatively sparsely populated area. Also at Essendine the branch lines from Stamford East and from Bourne connected with East Coast main line services via local trains to Grantham or Peterborough North.

The short line to Stamford East had opened as early as 1856 as the Stamford & Essendine Railway and became part of the GNR in 1893, though the GNR had worked its trains for many years. The normal engines were ex-GNR tanks, latterly 'C12s', but these were replaced at the end by ex-GCR 'N5' tanks. There was a small engine shed at Stamford East, beside the River Welland, where the branch engines were stabled.

The Essendine to Bourne line was the first to close in 1951. The closure of Essendine station and the 4 miles of line to Stamford East followed in 1959; Stamford East station had closed in March 1957 and Essendine trains were thereafter diverted to the Midland station at Stamford Town. To the end, there was a small intermediate station on the GNR line at Ryhall, 2¼ miles from Stamford East.

Right:
The railways of Rutland.

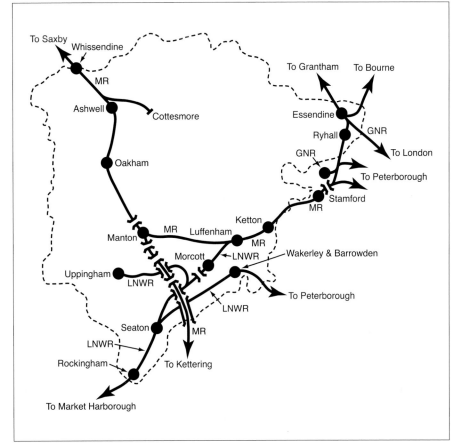

To Saxby
Whissendine
MR
Ashwell
Cottesmore
Oakham
Manton
MR
Luffenham
Ketton
MR
Morcott
LNWR
Wakerley & Barrowden
Uppingham
LNWR
Seaton
LNWR
MR
Rockingham
To Kettering
To Market Harborough
To Grantham
To Bourne
Essendine
GNR
Ryhall
GNR
To London
Stamford
MR
To Peterborough
To Peterborough
LNWR

Below:
On a very frosty Sunday morning in December 1957, 'Jubilee' No 45610, then still named *Gold Coast*, passes Ashwell station at speed. The train is from Nottingham Midland to London St Pancras via Melton Mowbray and Manton. *D. W. Webb*

Left:
Seaton Tunnel (208 yards) is about to be entered by Toton '8F' No 48303 pulling an ironstone train from Northamptonshire northwards on 13 June 1959. *J. M. Mason*

Below left:
The push-and-pull Stamford train is in the bay platform at Seaton in the summer of 1962. The engine is Ivatt 2-6-2 tank No 41225. *D. W. Webb*

Right:
A contrast between LNWR and BR signals at the north end of Seaton station in May 1959: the left-hand signals are for the Uppingham and Stamford bay and the right set for the main lines through the station. From left to right, the arms relate to the Uppingham, Stamford and Peterborough routes. *D. W. Webb*

Right:
The LNWR arm for Uppingham is 'off' as LMS 4-4-2 tank No 41975 leaves the bay platform at Seaton with its single-coach train in May 1959. A fine old lamp stands on the left and cattle pens are seen in the goods yard. *D. W. Webb*

Left:
On 13 June 1959 the morning mixed train has just left Seaton for Uppingham and is passing under the Manton to Kettering line. After a further mile, the Uppingham line passed back under the Manton line and headed west to the terminus. The other track, in the foreground, went to Luffenham Junction via Morcott and was used by Stamford trains. *J. M. Mason*

Right:
An RCTS special, led by a 2-6-4 tank and pushed by 4F class 0-6-0 No 44414, heads up the branch to Uppingham on 18 May 1963; the other line is the Luffenham Junction route via Morcott. The train was too long to be run round at Uppingham, so an engine was coupled to each end. *D. W. Webb*

Left:
The single-coach Uppingham train, behind LMS-built 4-4-2 tank No 41975, has just come back under the Manton to Kettering line heading for the branch terminus on 27 May 1958. *M. Mason*

Above:
No 41975 is about to leave Uppingham for Seaton on the same day. The goods yard is quite busy and the whole station area is neat and tidy. The run-round loop is in the foreground. Signals and points were worked from a ground frame in the open behind the engine, as there was no signalbox. *M. Mason*

Right:
One and a half passengers have just arrived at Morcott station after shopping at Stamford on a winter's afternoon in 1962. The 2-6-2 tank at the rear has just started to propel its train on the final leg of its journey to Seaton. *D. W. Webb*

Left:
A Seaton to Stamford train has just left the single-line approach to Luffenham Junction on 9 June 1962. One of the arms on this fine Midland Railway signal is 'off' for the platform loop at the nearby South Luffenham station. Class 2P 2-6-2 tank No 41271 was one of the engines fitted for 'motor' working. *J. M. Mason*

Right:
Between passenger duties on the Stamford Town to Essendine trains, Class N5 0-6-2 tank No 69266 spent some time shunting the busy goods yard at Stamford Town. The large MR goods shed is behind the engine and wagons in this May 1959 picture. The brake-van is one of the LNER-built vehicles on which the BR standard brake-vans were based. *D. W. Webb*

Left:
Class C12 4-4-2 tank No 67398 stands at the tiny station at Ryhall on 2 August 1958. The train is the 6.20pm from Stamford East, due at Essendine at 6.30pm. *J. M. Mason*

Above:
An afternoon train from Stamford East approaches Essendine on 26 July 1958 pulled by Class N5 No 69274. *M. Mason*

Below:
'Essendine Change for Stamford' says the station name board in September 1958. A short goods train from Stamford East has just arrived behind Class C12 No 67398. *J. M. Mason*

Left:
United Steel Companies opened Exton Park ironstone quarries in 1951, and ten brand new locomotives were supplied by Yorkshire Engine Co. These powerful 0-6-0s were well maintained, but had a surprisingly short life, being replaced by new diesels in the mid-1960s. An excavator loads iron ore into a train of tippler wagons headed by one of the Yorkshire engines on 19 May 1964. The quarries closed in 1973. *D. W. Webb*

Below:
The full length of the magnificent Welland Viaduct is seen as preserved Class A3 Pacific No 4472 *Flying Scotsman* crosses with an up GMRS special on 11 September 1965. *J. M. Mason*